BEASTLY BOOKS FOR THE BRAVE

THIS BOOK
CHARGES!

SARAH MACHAJEWSKI

Gareth Stevens
PUBLISHING

Please visit our website, www.garethstevens.com. For a free color catalog of all our high-quality books, call toll free 1-800-542-2595 or fax 1-877-542-2596.

Cataloging-in-Publication Data

Names: Machajewski, Sarah.
Title: This book charges! / Sarah Machajewski.
Description: New York : Gareth Stevens Publishing, 2020. | Series: Beastly books for the brave | Includes glossary and index.
Identifiers: ISBN 9781538233559 (pbk.) | ISBN 9781538233573 (library bound) | ISBN 9781538233566 (6pack)
Subjects: LCSH: Animal locomotion--Juvenile literature. | Animals--Adaptations--Juvenile literature. | Speed--Juvenile literature.
Classification: LCC QP310.R85 M23 2020 | DDC 591.5'7--dc23

First Edition

Published in 2020 by
Gareth Stevens Publishing
111 East 14th Street, Suite 349
New York, NY 10003

Copyright © 2020 Gareth Stevens Publishing

Designer: Katelyn E. Reynolds
Editor: Kate Light

Photo credits: Cover, p. 1 (bull) Raimund Linke/Photodisc/Getty Images; cover, pp. 1-24 (book cover) Ensuper/Shutterstock.com; cover, p. 1-24 (tape) Picsfive/Shutterstock.com; cover, pp. 1-24 (decorative elements) cute vector art/Shutterstock.com; cover, pp. 1-24 (book interior and wood background) robert_s/Shutterstock.com; p. 4-21 (fun fact background) Miloje/Shutterstock.com; pp. 5, 21 (rhino) neelsky/Shutterstock.com; pp. 7, 21 (bighorn ram) AL PARKER PHOTOGRAPHY/Shutterstock.com; pp. 9 (main), 21 (elephant) aaltair/Shutterstock.com; p. 9 (inset) Pentium5/Shutterstock.com; pp. 11, 21 (bull) Shawn Hine/Shutterstock.com; p. 13 Kolbz/iStock Unreleased/Getty Images; pp. 15 (main), 21 (bear) Warren Metcalf/Shutterstock.com; p. 15 (inset) Scott E Read/Shutterstock.com; p. 16 Jez Bennett/Shutterstock.com; pp. 17, 21 (lion) Mogens Trolle/Shutterstock.com; p. 18 Tanya Puntti/Shutterstock.com; pp. 19, 21 (gorilla) Ronan Donovan/National Geographic/Getty Images; pp. 20, 21 (hippo) Thomas Dressler/Gallo Images/Getty Images.

Printed in the United States of America

CPSIA compliance information: Batch #CS19GS: For further information contact Gareth Stevens, New York, New York at 1-800-542-2595.

CONTENTS

WORDS IN THE GLOSSARY APPEAR IN **BOLD** TYPE THE FIRST TIME THEY ARE USED IN THE TEXT.

PROCEED WITH CAUTION

So, you want to learn about charging animals? Animals that charge can be very dangerous, you know. Imagine you're out in the wild and you see a rhinoceros in the distance. All of a sudden, the rhino turns—and starts running right at you! Are you sure you want to read on?

Charging is a beastly behavior that only the bravest readers can handle. If you're up to the challenge, here's your chance to see animals on the move. Just stay out of their way!

GET OUT OF THE WAY OF THE CHARGING BEASTS IN THIS BOOK!

BEASTLY BASICS

Out here in the wild kingdom, it's every animal for itself. Some animals are predators, which means they eat other animals. Animals that get eaten by other animals are called prey. Predators and prey have developed **adaptations** that help their species, or kind, survive over time.

Some animals have adapted to charge when they sense danger nearby. This **aggressive behavior** tells the **threat** to get lost. Other animals use charging to hunt. Charging at full speed helps them catch fast-moving prey.

FACTS FOR THE FEARLESS

SOME ANIMALS FIGHT BY CHARGING INTO EACH OTHER! MALE BIGHORN SHEEP, CALLED RAMS, FIGHT TO SEE WHO GETS TO BE IN CHARGE OF THE GROUP.

BIGHORN SHEEP EARNED THEIR NAME FOR A REASON. A SET OF RAM'S HORNS CAN WEIGH UP TO 30 POUNDS (13.6 KG)!

ANGRY ELEPHANTS

Look at this enormous elephant! You may think an animal this size doesn't fear anything, but lions, tigers, and hyenas sometimes try to attack elephants.

Elephants show aggressive behavior when they're faced with a threat. Angry elephants stomp their large feet, shake their huge heads, and make noises with their trunks. And when they get really mad, they charge at full speed. Elephants can run up to 15 miles (24 km) per hour. That means a predator has to get out of the way, fast!

FACTS FOR THE FEARLESS

ELEPHANTS GET EXTRA ANGRY IF THEIR CALVES, OR BABIES, ARE IN DANGER. THEY CHARGE TO KEEP THEIR CALVES SAFE FROM PREDATORS ON THE HUNT.

MOTHER ELEPHANT PROTECTING BABY

WHAT IS AN ELEPHANT'S BIGGEST THREAT? HUMANS.
ELEPHANTS HAVE BEEN KNOWN TO
CHARGE PEOPLE WHO ENTER THEIR **HABITAT.**

CHARGING BULLS

Can a cow charge you? If it's angry, it sure can! Male cows are called bulls, and bulls are known for charging. They charge when they're **agitated** or to show **dominance**.

When a bull is mad, it will lower its head and shoulders. It may shake its head, snort, or start pawing at the dirt with its hoof. These are all warning signs that it may charge. Running at full speed, the bull is sure to hurt anything in its path with its huge horns.

FACTS FOR THE FEARLESS

IT'S COMMONLY THOUGHT THAT BULLS CHARGE WHEN THEY SEE THE COLOR RED, BUT THEY ACTUALLY CHARGE WHEN THEY SEE SUDDEN MOVEMENTS OR OTHER THREATS.

You don't want to be near a bull showing signs of aggressive behavior—it might charge!

RAGING RHINOS

See this large beast with stonelike skin and a huge, sharp horn? It's a rhinoceros, and it won't **hesitate** to charge!

Charging is the rhino's defense against predators, and it will charge at just about anything. That's because rhinos can't see very well. They can only see about 90 feet (27.4 m) in front of them, so they can't really tell if something is a threat. That's why you see rhinos charge at trees, rocks, or even cars!

FACTS FOR THE FEARLESS

A GROUP OF RHINOS IS CALLED A CRASH. FOR THESE CHARGING BEASTS, THAT SEEMS LIKE THE PERFECT WORD!

RHINOS CAN RUN UP TO **40** MILES (**64.4** KM) PER HOUR. EVEN IN A CAR, HUMANS NEED TO BE CAREFUL AROUND THESE FAST BEASTS!

BLUFFING BEARS

The bear is another wild beast that is known to charge. Like elephants, bears will charge when they feel threatened, especially when it comes to protecting their babies.

However, most bear charges don't turn into full-on attacks. Bears have been known to charge and then turn away at the last second. This behavior is called bluffing. It's meant to scare away the threat. Bears will also snap their jaws, snarl, or stomp their feet to show they're agitated.

FACTS FOR THE FEARLESS

BEAR ATTACKS ON HUMANS ARE RARE, OR UNCOMMON. STILL, IT'S NEVER BRAVE TO MESS WITH A WILD ANIMAL.

CHARGING, EVEN WHEN IT'S A BLUFF, SENDS THE MESSAGE THAT THE BEAR IS BIGGER AND STRONGER THAN ITS THREAT.

15

LIONS ON THE ATTACK

So far, you've bravely read about beasts that charge to defend themselves. Are you ready to meet some fearsome creatures that charge to attack? Lions are one killer example!

When lions hunt, they like to **ambush** their prey. This involves a behavior called stalking. The lion follows its prey from a distance, moving slowly and quietly. Then, it attacks! The lion leaps out of hiding and charges its prey at full speed. Sometimes, lions hunt together by circling their prey and charging all at once.

LION PRIDE ATTACKS A BUFFALO

FEMALE LIONS DO MOST OF THE HUNTING. THEY CAN RUN UP TO **50** MILES (**80.5** KM) PER HOUR, BUT ONLY FOR A SHORT TIME.

GORILLAS IN CHARGE

Sometimes, charging is used to show other animals who's the boss. For gorillas, charging is part of the fight to show dominance. They fight to defend their position in the group. Would you be brave enough to watch?

Gorillas also charge when they feel threatened or attacked. They'll start by beating their chest, biting, and scratching. If they feel really threatened, they'll charge. Like bears, they may bluff and turn away at the last second. It's a **tactic** used to scare off the threat.

GORILLA BEATING ITS CHEST

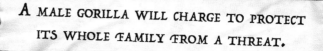

A MALE GORILLA WILL CHARGE TO PROTECT ITS WHOLE FAMILY FROM A THREAT.

INTO THE BRAVE UNKNOWN

You made it to the end of this beastly book without being crushed by a charging animal! But there are other charging creatures to meet, and some are even more deadly than the beasts you've already survived. You might have thought lions were bad, but hippos are even more dangerous. They'll run straight at humans who enter their habitat.

What other beasts are waiting to charge? It's up to you to find out—if you dare!

ANGRY HIPPO CHARGING

Why Do Animals Charge?

BULL
- ☑ TO DEFEND
- ☐ TO HUNT
- ☑ TO SHOW DOMINANCE

HIPPO
- ☐ TO DEFEND
- ☐ TO HUNT
- ☑ TO SHOW DOMINANCE

BIGHORN RAM
- ☐ TO DEFEND
- ☐ TO HUNT
- ☑ TO SHOW DOMINANCE

LION
- ☐ TO DEFEND
- ☑ TO HUNT
- ☐ TO SHOW DOMINANCE

BEAR
- ☑ TO DEFEND
- ☐ TO HUNT
- ☐ TO SHOW DOMINANCE

GORILLA
- ☑ TO DEFEND
- ☐ TO HUNT
- ☑ TO SHOW DOMINANCE

RHINO
- ☑ TO DEFEND
- ☐ TO HUNT
- ☐ TO SHOW DOMINANCE

ELEPHANT
- ☑ TO DEFEND
- ☐ TO HUNT
- ☐ TO SHOW DOMINANCE

SOME ANIMALS CHARGE FOR MORE THAN ONE REASON!

GLOSSARY

adaptation: a change in a type of animal that makes it better able to live in its surroundings

aggressive: showing a readiness to attack

agitate: to bother

ambush: a surprise attack. Also, to attack from a hiding place.

behavior: the way an animal acts

dominance: the state of being the most powerful or strongest

habitat: the natural place where an animal or plant lives

hesitate: to pause before doing something

tactic: a method for accomplishing a goal

threat: something likely to cause harm

FOR MORE INFORMATION

BOOKS

Spilsbury, Louise and Richard Spilsbury. *Animal Adaptations.* Minneapolis, MN: Bellwether Media, Inc. 2017.

Tracosas, L.J. *Predators: Discover 20 of Nature's Most Ferocious Hunters.* Bellevue, WA: becker&mayer! kids, 2017.

Waldron, Melanie. *Adaptation.* Chicago, IL: Capstone Heinemann Library, 2014.

WEBSITES

Animal Adaptations & Characteristics – PBS Kids
ny.pbslearningmedia.org/collection/adaptations/2/
Learn about different animal adaptations through cool videos!

San Diego Zoo
zoo.sandiegozoo.org
The San Diego Zoo provides engaging information on all kinds of animals and their behavior.

Study Jams
studyjams.scholastic.com/studyjams/jams/science/animals/animal-adaptations.htm
Test your knowledge of animal adaptations at this interactive site.

INDEX